Soft Skills Sleuths

COMMUNICATION

INVESTIGATING LIFE SKILLS SUCCESS

Diane L   ansen

Published in the United States of America by Cherry Lake Publishing Group
Ann Arbor, Michigan
www.cherrylakepublishing.com

Created and produced by Bright Futures Press
www.brightfuturespress.com

Reading Advisor: Marla Conn, MS, Ed., Literacy specialist, Read-Ability, Inc.
Illustrator: Ruth Bennett
Cover and Page Designer: Kathy Heming
Design Elements: © mijatmijatovic/Shutterstock.com; © GoodStudio/Shutterstock.com;
    © Denis Cristo/Shutterstock.com; © Lorelyn Medina/Shutterstock.com; © Yaroshenko Olena/
    Shutterstock.com; © rangsan paidaen/Shutterstock.com

Copyright ©2021 by Cherry Lake Publishing Group
All rights reserved. No part of this book may be reproduced or utilized in any form or by any means
without written permission from the publisher.

Cherry Lake Press is an imprint of Cherry Lake Publishing Group.

Library of Congress Cataloging-in-Publication Data has been filed and is available at catalog.loc.gov

Cherry Lake Publishing Group would like to acknowledge the work of the Partnership for 21st Century
Learning, a Network of Battelle for Kids. Please visit http://www.battelleforkids.org/networks/p21
for more information.

Printed in the United States of America
Corporate Graphics

TABLE OF CONTENTS

What Are Soft Skills and
   Why Do I Need Them? 4

Chapter 1 Soft Skill #1: Listening 6

Chapter 2 Soft Skill #2: Talking 12

Chapter 3 Soft Skill #3: Body Language 18

Chapter 4 Soft Skill #4: Writing 24

Communication Quiz 30

Glossary 31

Index 32

About the Authors 32

About the Illustrator 32

What Are Soft Skills and

Skills are needed to succeed at any job you can imagine. Different jobs require different skills. Professional baseball players need good batting and catching skills. Brain surgeons need steady hands and lots of practice with a scalpel. These are examples of **hard skills** necessary to do specific jobs.

Everyone needs "**soft skills**" to succeed in life. Soft skills get personal. They are about how you behave and treat people. Soft skills are the skills you need to be the very best *you* at home, work, and school.

"Sounds good," you say. "But I don't have a job. Why do I need to worry about soft skills?"

Ahh, but you do have a job. In fact, you have a very important job. You are a student, and your job is to learn as much as you can. Learning soft skills makes you a better student now. It also gets you ready to succeed in any career you choose later.

Communication soft skills help you hear and be heard. In this book, you get to be a soft skills **sleuth**. You will track down clues about what good (and not so good!) communication skills look like. You will **investigate** four communication soft skills cases:

- **Listening**
- **Talking**
- **Body Language**
- **Writing**

Why Do I Need Them?

HOW TO USE THIS BOOK

Here's how you can be a soft skills sleuth. In each chapter:

 Gather the facts. Read the description about the soft skill.

 Read the case file. Check out a situation where soft skills are needed.

 Investigate the case. Look for clues showing soft skills *successes* and soft skills *mistakes*. Keep track of the clues on a blank sheet of paper.

 Crack the case. Did you spot all the clues?

SOFT SKILL #1····

It is one thing to hear what someone says. It is another thing to **listen** to what they mean. Ears pick up sound all the time. That's what ears do. Hearing a sound doesn't equal listening to it. Listening is a choice. You decide to focus and pay attention.

When teachers say "listen up!" they are asking you make that choice. Listening is a skill you can learn, practice, and improve.

Listening is a key to learning. It is how you make sense of new information. It is how you get instructions and figure out rules. When you listen to other people talk, you get to know them. It is how you make new friends. Good listeners know more. They get along better with other people. Good listeners enjoy greater success at home, at school, and on the job.

Do **These Things** to be a **Good Listener**

- Look at the speaker.
- Relax and focus your attention.
- Ignore distractions.
- Listen for meaning.
- Picture in your mind what the speaker is saying.
- Ask questions when you don't understand.
- Wait for speaker to pause before adding comments.
- Show interest by nodding, smiling, and other gestures.
- Take notes to help you remember.

"We have two ears and one mouth so we can listen twice as much as speak."

—Epictetus

LISTENING

SOFT SKILLS CASE #1: LISTENING

There is a big test on Friday! Today is review day. Miss Bevens is explaining what the **students** need to know. Mind you, it is fifth period and it has been a long day. It is a challenge to focus on such a beautiful spring day.

Some students are showing listening success. Others are not. Turn the page and take a look. Can you spot the good listeners? What are they doing? How can you tell that some of the students are not paying attention to Miss Bevens?

DO:
Investigate listening successes and mistakes!

DO NOT:
Write in this book!

Take a look at this classroom scene. It is pretty clear that some of these students will be ready for the test on Friday and some will not.

IS EVERYONE LISTENING TO MISS BEVENS?

LISTENING

What did your investigation uncover? Did you spot successful listeners? In what ways are other students making listening mistakes?

Did you **find** all the successes and **MISTAKES**?

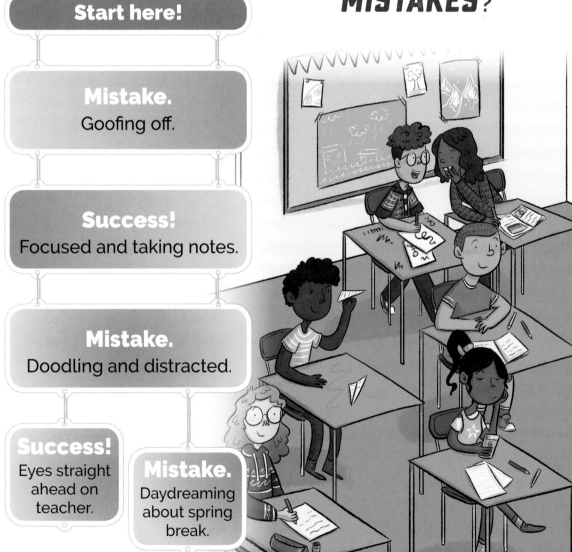

Start here!

Mistake.
Goofing off.

Success!
Focused and taking notes.

Mistake.
Doodling and distracted.

Success!
Eyes straight ahead on teacher.

Mistake.
Daydreaming about spring break.

CASE NOTES

How can you improve your listening skills?

Success! Asking good questions.

Mistake. Cell phone in class? Oh no!

Did you find them all?

Success! Giving feedback.

Mistake. When you snooze, you lose.

Success! Sitting straight and still.

Mistake. Chatting and not paying attention.

Success! Smiling and showing respect for teacher.

SOFT SKILL #2

Talking, or **verbal communication**, is how you make yourself heard. It is how you use words to express your needs. Talking is how you share ideas. Talking lets you express who you are and what you think. Good verbal communication is one part talking and one part listening.

Finding your "voice" is an important part of growing up. Speaking up when the time is right is a big deal. Others will listen when you speak with respect and **confidence**.

Sometimes it can be a little scary to talk in front of groups of people. Just remember that what you have to say is just as important as what others are saying. Speak up, speak out, and don't forget to listen to what others are saying too.

For many jobs, talking to an employer is one of the first steps in getting hired. The way you express yourself makes a strong first impression. Make sure your first impression is a good one!

Do These Things to Be a Good Talker

- Think before you speak.
- Speak clearly in a strong voice.
- Speak calmly even when you are upset.
- Say what needs to be said in as few words as possible.
- Avoid talking too much; instead, listen more.
- Use positive words to show interest in what others are saying.
- Say what you mean and mean what you say.

"Wise men talk because they have something to say; fools, because they have to say something."
—Plato

TALKING

SOFT SKILLS CASE #2: TALKING

It's time for the school soccer championship game. If only the two teams could agree on the rules! Everyone has their own ideas—and their own way to communicate them. Some of the players are using winning talking skills. They are speaking clearly and kindly. They are sticking to the point and sharing good ideas.

There are also some losing skills at play here. Some of the students are making more noise than they are making sense. Others are tuned out and not contributing to the discussion. Can you spot the winners and losers, and get this game started?

DO:
Investigate talking successes and mistakes!

DO NOT:
Write in this book!

There is a lot at stake in this championship game. Before the game starts, the players have to make sure the rules are fair and square. May the best talking skills win!

TALKING

What kinds of talking skills did you spot? Who is winning the communication game with successful talking skills?

Did you **find** all the successes and **MISTAKES**?

Start here!

Mistake.
Whoa! Turn the volume down!

Success!
Hey, let's talk about this.

Mistake.
Leaving people out of the conversation.

Mistake.
Bullying to get your own way.

CASE NOTES

Mistake.
Huh?
Speak up!

Success!
High five!
We worked
it out.

Have you found your voice yet?

Did you find them all?

Success!
Listen up, everyone.
Speaking up to
get the conversation
back on track.

Mistake.
Tuning out and letting
others decide the rules.

Mistake.
Gossiping about the
other team.

SOFT SKILL #3

Sometimes you say a lot without speaking a single word. Other times your words say one thing while your expressions say something else. That's because your **body language** is coming through loud and clear! Body language is also called **nonverbal communication**.

Facial expressions, hand gestures, and posture are some of the ways your body "talks." Eyes often provide strong clues about what a person is really thinking or feeling. Maybe your teachers or parents have "the look." Just one glance and you know that you are in big trouble!

Sometimes you don't even realize what your body is saying. Has your parent or teacher ever said "Don't look at me that way!" That usually means your bad attitude is showing.

Of course, body language also says good things. Imagine the look on someone's face when they are happy to see you. Think about the way your favorite sports team celebrates after winning a big game. Body language tells the story!

The thing about body language is that you give it *and* you receive it. Pay attention, and make sure you are sending and receiving the right messages.

When Your Body Talks

- Your face shows your **emotions**. It says "happy," "angry," "sad," "afraid," "excited," "bored," and more.

- Your hands send messages. Thumbs up ("good"). Thumbs down ("bad"). High five ("yes!"). "Come here." "Go away."

- Arms crossed in front of your body says "I'm so not into this."

- Hands on hips say "I mean business!"

"Your body communicates as well as your mouth. Don't contradict yourself."
—Allen Ruddock

BODY LANGUAGE

SOFT SKILLS CASE #3: BODY LANGUAGE

Uh-oh. A prankster is on the loose in math class. He or she is causing all kinds of funny—and very distracting—**chaos**. But enough is enough. Mr. Austin, the school principal, has "invited" the students in the math class into his office. He wants to find out what is going on.

Before starting the discussion, the principal looks at everyone's body language. It seems like each student is conveying a different message: worried, tuned out, helpful, sassy. Each student's body language is making their feelings heard loud and clear.

What is their body language saying? Is anyone's body language saying "guilty"?

DO:
Investigate body language successes and mistakes!

DO NOT:
Write in this book!

BODY LANGUAGE

There are several different messages being sent by the students in the principal's office. Can you "read" what they are saying?

Did you **find** all the successes and **MISTAKES**?

Start here!

Success!
Confident and helpful, someone is getting right to the point.

Mistake.
Scared and guilty? Or just stressed out?

Success!
Mr. Austin means business!

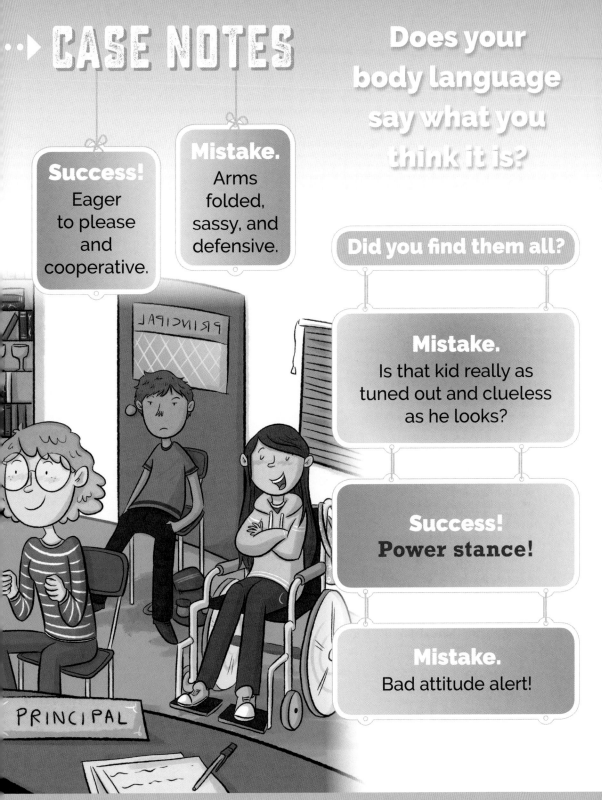

SOFT SKILL #4

Did you know that history is impossible without written language? The earliest humans left evidence of their way of life in drawings made in caves. Today more than 2.2 million new books are published worldwide every year. How many books is this? According to the late and brilliant physicist Stephen Hawking, "If you stacked the new books published next to each other ... you would have to move at 90 miles an hour just to keep up with the end of the line." That's a lot of written communication!

As a student, your **writing** skills come into play every day on essay tests, book reports, and other assignments. You may also use writing skills after school in texts and emails and other **social media**. When you grow up and start your career, good writing skills may spell the difference between a good job and a great one.

Writing is one of the main ways that people share information and ideas with other people. Good writing lets people (like teachers and employers) know that you know what you need to know.

Do These Things to be a Good Writer

- Remember that all good writers are also good readers.
- Edit your work every time. All good writing is rewriting!
- Read what you write out loud (or in your head) to make sure that it makes sense.
- Spell-check everything you write.
- Avoid using big words when small words will do.
- Say what you mean and stop.

"If you want to change the world, pick up your pen and write."
—Martin Luther

WRITING

SOFT SKILLS CASE #4: WRITING

In the first writing lesson of the new school year, Ms. Fry explained how important it is for writers to edit their work. She said that "good writing is rewriting." Then she asked the class to write a short report about "what I did for summer vacation."

The students' parents will be visiting the class later that evening. So the reports are a big deal. Ms. Fry wants to show off their work on the bulletin board.

To sweeten the deal, Ms. Fry is giving students who use good writing skills an extra recess. Those who don't do this will have to stay inside and try again. Can you tell which students deserve extra goof-off time? Which ones need a do-over?

DO:
Investigate writing successes and mistakes!

DO NOT:
Write in this book!

WHO IS WRITING THE RIGHT WAY?

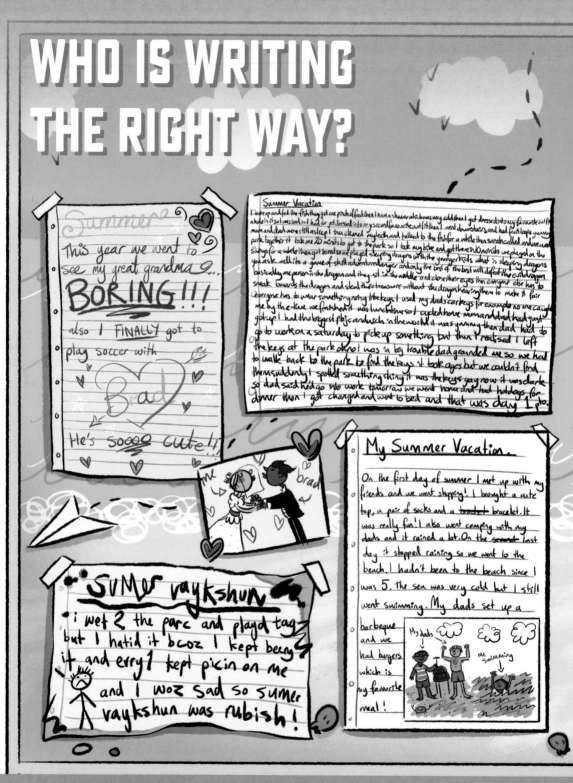

Note 1:

Summer

This year we went to see my great grandma... **BORING!!!**

also I FINALLY got to play soccer with **Brad**

He's soooo cute!!!

Note 2:

Summer Vacation

I woke up and fed the fish they got one pinch of food then I have a shower which was very cold then I get dressed into my favourite outfit a halo ship so I was sad so I had to get dressed into my scruff you ain't scruff then I went downstairs and had first loops yummy mum and dad were still asleep I then cleaned myself and talked to the fish for a while then a sarah called ashlee went to the park together it took me 20 minits to get to the park so I took my bike and got there in 10 minits we played on the swings for a while then got bored so we played sleeping dragons with the younger kids what is sleeping dragons you ask well it's a game of skill adventure danger and only the best of the best will defeat the evil dragon basically one person is the dragon and they sit in the middle and close their eyes then everyone else has to sneak towards the dragon and steal their treasure without the dragon hearing them to make it fair everyone has to wear something noisy like keys I used my dads car keys for example no one caught me by the time we finished it was lunch time so I cycled home mum and dad had just got up I had the biggest pb jjs sandwich in the world it was yummy then dad had to go to work on a saturday to pick up something but then I realised I left the keys at the park oh no I was in big trouble dad grounded me so we had to walk back to the park to find the keys it took ages but we couldn't find them suddenly I spotted something shiny it was the keys yay now it was dark so dad said he'd go into work tomorrow we went home and had hotdogs for dinner then I got changed and went to bed and that was day 1 pto.

Note 3:

Sumer vaykshun

i wet 2 the parc and playd tag but I hatid it bcoz I kept beeng it and erry1 kept picin on me and I woz sad so sumer vaykshun was rubish!

Note 4:

My Summer Vacation.

On the first day of summer I met up with my friends and we went shopping! I brought a cute top, a pair of socks and a bracelet. It was really fun! I also went camping with my dads and it rained a lot. On the last day it stopped raining so we went to the beach. I hadn't been to the beach since I was 5. The sea was very cold but I still went swimming. My dads set up a barbeque and we had burgers which is my favourite meal!

Which students earned an extra recess? Which students had to stay inside to rewrite and revise?

Did you **find** all the successes and **MISTAKES**?

Start here!

Mistake.
Emails and school reports are two different things.

Success!
Descriptive and nicely illustrated!

Mistake.
Spell check needed!

Summer!
This year we went to see my great grandma
BORING!!!
I FINALLY got to soccer with
Bad
t's soooo Cute!!!

Summer Vacation

My Summer Vacation.

On the first day of summer I met up with my friends and we went shopping! I brought a cute top, a pair of socks and a bracelet. It was really fun! I also went camping with my dads and it rained a lot. On the second last day it stopped raining so we went to the beach. I hadn't been to the beach since I was 5. The sea was very cold but I still went swimming. My dads set up a barbeque and we had burgers which is my favourite meal!

Sumer vaykshun
I wet 2 the parc and playd tag but I hatid it bcoz I kept beeng it and erry1 kept picin on me and I woz sad so sumer vaykshun was rubish!

CASE NOTES

Do you have the write stuff?

Mistake.
Excuse me, but your bad attitude is showing.

Success!
Nice, neat, and to the point.

Did you find them all?

Mistake.
It helps to follow the instructions.

Mistake.
TMI =
Too much information!

Mistake.
Focus on topic not Brad.

WHAT HAVE YOU Learned? ·······▶ COMMUNICATION QUIZ

Question 1:

Every person needs
___ ___ for
every job.

Question 2:

Listening, talking,
body language,
and writing
are examples
of important
___ skills.

Question 3:

Good listeners
make a ___
to listen.

Question 4:

Good verbal
communication
is one part
___
and one part
___.

Question 5:

You ___
and ___
body language.

Question 6:

Your face expresses
your ___.

Question 7:

Writing confirms
___.

Question 8:

All good writing is
___.

ANSWERS

1. *soft skills*
2. *communication*
3. *choice*
4. *talking, listening*
5. *send, receive*
6. *emotions (or feelings)*
7. *knowledge or understanding*
8. *rewriting*

Communication soft skills start here!

GLOSSARY

body language (BAH-dee LANG-gwij) gestures and movements a person's face or body makes that convey messages

chaos (kā-ŏs) total disorder and confusion; mayhem

confidence (KAHN-fih-duhns) having a strong belief in your own abilities

emotions (ih-MOH-shuhnz) feelings such as love, happiness, or anger

hard skills (HAHRD SKILZ) specific skills needed to do a specific job

investigate (in-VES-tih-gate) to gather information or clues about something

listen (LIS-uhn) to choose to hear something on purpose

nonverbal communication (nahn-VUR-buhl kuh-myoo-nih-KAY-shuhn) sharing information without words by way of facial expressions, touching, tone of voice, posture, and other actions

power stance (POU-ur STANS) the firm way someone stands that shows they are in command

sleuth (SLOOTH) a detective, or person who is good at finding facts and clues

social media (SOH-shuhl MEE-dee-uh) websites and computer programs that let people communicate and share information online

soft skills (SAWFT SKILZ) behaviors and personality traits people use every day to succeed in life

talking (TAWK-ing) using words to speak

verbal communication (VUR-buhl kuh-myoo-nih-KAY-shuhn) sharing information by using sounds and words

writing (RITE-ing) putting words on paper or in a digital format

INDEX

emotions, 18

Epictetus, 6

hard skills, 4

Hawking, Stephen, 24

Luther, Martin, 24

nonverbal communication, 18

power stance, 18

Plato, 12

Ruddock, Allen, 18

social media, 24

verbal communication, 12

ABOUT THE AUTHORS ◄ • • • • • • • • • • • • • • •

Diane Lindsey Reeves likes to write books that help students figure out what they want to be when they grow up. She mostly lives in Washington, D.C., but spends as much time as she can in North Carolina and South Carolina with her grandkids.

Connie Hansen spent 25 years teaching college students about successful life skills. She lives in Lynchburg, Virginia where her favorite thing to do is play with her grandchildren. Her happy place is the beach!

• • • • • • • • • • • • • ► ABOUT THE ILLUSTRATOR

Ruth Bennett lives in a small country village in the heart of Norfolk, England, with her two cats, Queen Elizabeth and Queen Victoria. She loves petting dogs, watching movies, and drawing, of course!